DRAW 50

FLOWERS, TREES
AND OTHER PLANTS

DRAW 50
FLOWERS, TREES AND OTHER PLANTS

LEE J. AMES with P. LEE AMES

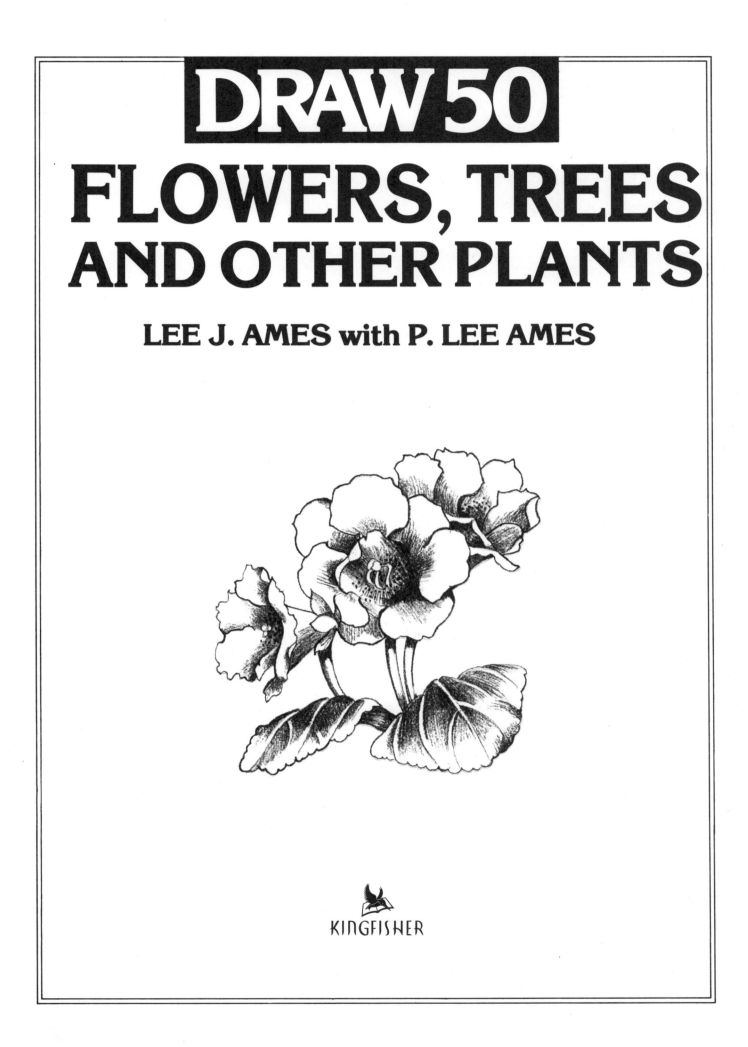

KINGFISHER

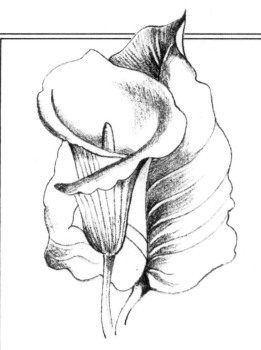

KINGFISHER
Kingfisher Publications Plc
New Penderel House, 283-288 High Holborn
London WC1V 7HZ
www.kingfisherpub.com

First published in Great Britian 1995
by Kingfisher Books
Published by arrangement with Doubleday,
a division of Bantam Doubleday Dell Publishing Group, Inc.

10 9 8 7 6 5 4 3 2 1

TS2/0504/AJT/CLSN/HBM//110WF-O/F

A CIP catalogue record for this book
is available from the British Library

ISBN 1 85697 469 3

Phototypeset by Southern Positives and Negatives (SPAN),
Lingfield, Surrey

Printed in India

To Jocelyn
who makes things
beautifully verdant . . .
always.

TO THE READER

To be able to see and enjoy what you are seeing is much to be grateful for. But even more, being able to reproduce and convey to others, by drawing, what you see or imagine provides greater satisfaction. As in all my books, my purpose and pleasure are to show others, like yourself, a way to construct drawings.

This world is full of glorious things to see. I think you'll agree that the flowers, fruits, trees and the rest of the subject matter here are testament to our beautiful world. In my earlier books, living subjects were all chosen from the animal kingdom. The other major kingdom in the tree of life is the vegetable kingdom, and almost all the drawings in this book are from there. The only exception is the mushroom, which is one of the fungi.

When you start working, I suggest you use clean white bond paper or drawing paper and a pencil with moderately soft lead (HB or No. 2). Keep a plastic, or 'putty' rubber handy (available at art supply shops). Choose the subject you want to draw and then, very lightly and carefully, sketch out the first step. Also very lightly and carefully, add the second step. As you go along, study not only the lines but the spaces between the lines. Size your first steps to fill your drawing paper well, not too large, not too small. Remember the first steps must be constructed with the greatest care. A mistake here could ruin the whole thing. As you work, it's a good idea to hold a mirror to your sketch from time to time. The image in the mirror frequently shows distortion you might not recognize otherwise.

You will notice that new step additions (in colour) are printed darker. This is so they can be clearly seen. But keep your construction steps always very light. Here's where the rubber can be useful. You can lighten a pencil stroke that is too dark by pressing on it with the rubber. When you've completed all the light steps, and when you're sure you have everything the way you want it, finish your drawing with firm, strong pencil lines. If you like, you can go over this with India ink (applied with a fine brush or pen) or a permanent fine-tipped ball-point pen or a felt-tipped marker. When the drawing is thoroughly dry, you can then use the rubber to clean off all the underlying pencil marks.

Remember, if your first attempts at drawing do not turn out the way you would like, it's important to *keep trying*. Your efforts will eventually pay off, and you will be pleased and surprised at what you can accomplish. I sincerely hope you will improve your drawing skills and have a great time drawing these beautiful plants.

Lee J. Ames

AUTHOR'S NOTE

In recent books, I have worked with artists whom I consider to be superbly talented. All are top achievers and craftspeople, highly acclaimed by their colleagues and fans . . . and some have names and work you may recognize. This way we are making available to you other styles of drawing, techniques that are different from my own. With that in mind, I consider myself very lucky to have been able to persuade Persis Lee Ames to join me in creating this book.

P. Lee Ames studied extensively at the Museum of Fine Arts in Boston and at the Art Students League in New York City. She then entered the commercial art field and developed a career in advertising, book illustration, jewellery design, and silver and greeting cards for Tiffany & Co. Now that her children are grown up, she works full-time on commissions for portraits, landscapes and murals for interior designers and private clients. Her work can be found in private collections here and in Europe, and has been featured in major magazines and newspapers.

Mrs Ames considers herself an illustrator of nature and a realistic painter. Flora is her speciality. She also excels in imaginative and whimsical *trompe l'oeil* and *faux* finishes. Recently she has studied at the Isabel O'Neil Studio in New York City, famed for its accomplishments in decorative arts. Her portrait paintings, murals and screens demonstrate the artistic talents of this truly Renaissance woman. And in case you're wondering, Persis and I are not related.

Lee J. Ames

Have fun with
your drawings . . .

Rose
Family: Rosaceae
Genus: *Rosa*

Daisy
Family: Compositae
Genus: *Chrysanthemum*

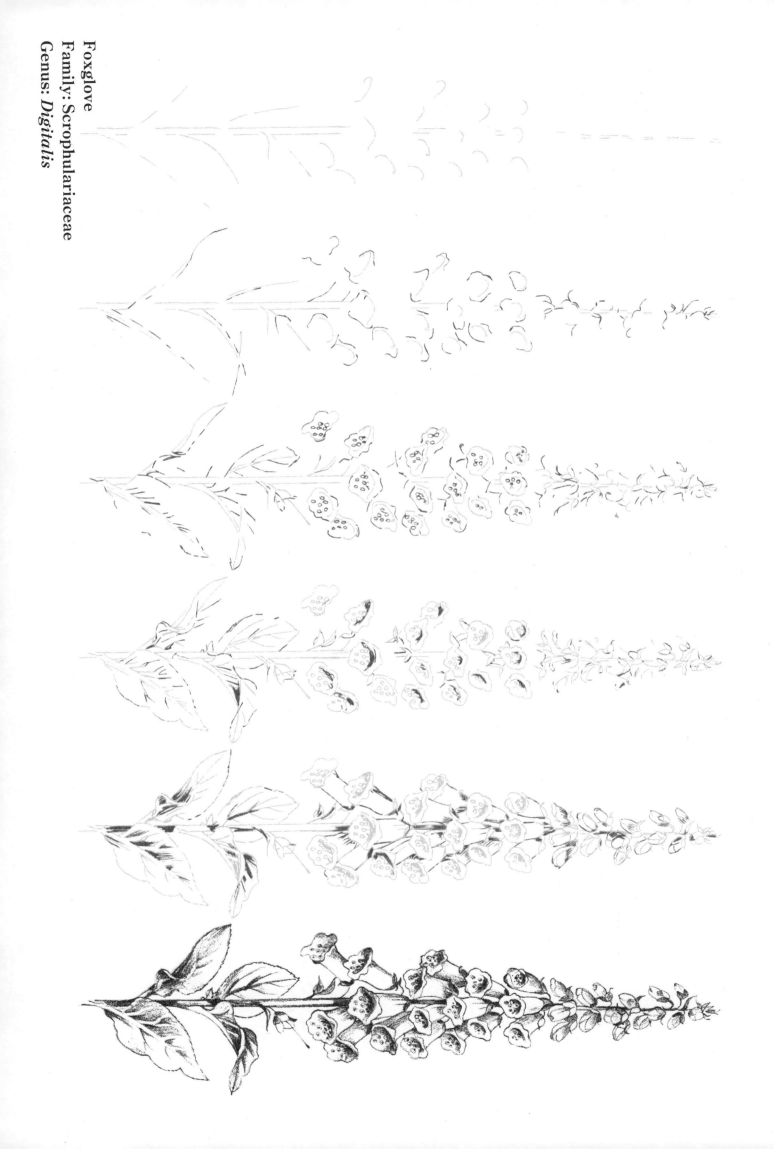

Foxglove
Family: Scrophulariaceae
Genus: *Digitalis*

Christmas cactus
Family: Cactaceae
Genus: *Schlumbergera*

White pine
Family: Pinaceae
Genus: *Pinus*

Passion flower
Family: Passifloraceae
Genus: *Passiflora*

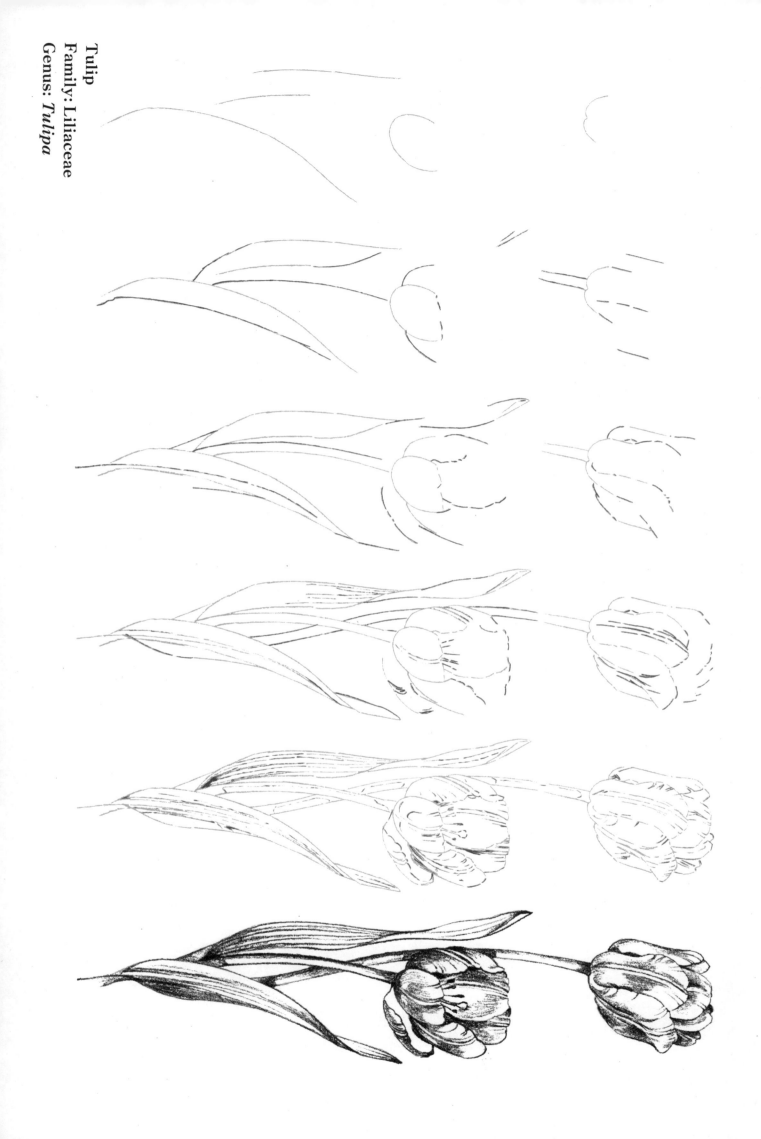

Tulip
Family: Liliaceae
Genus: *Tulipa*

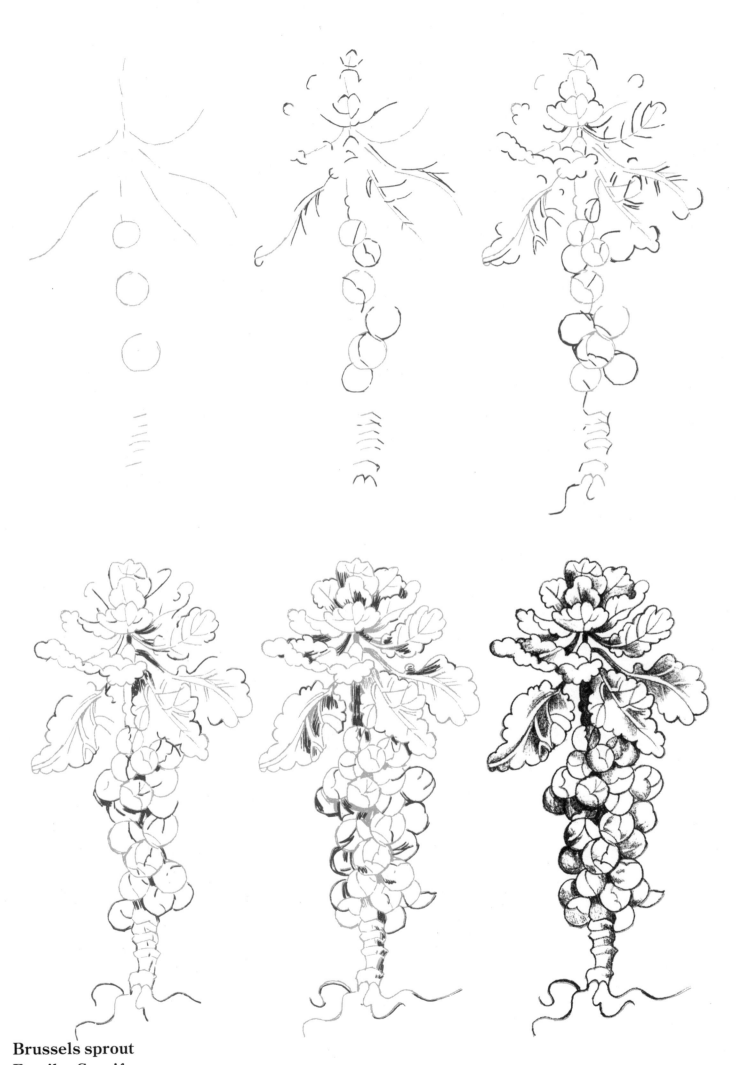

Brussels sprout
Family: Cruciferae
Genus: *Brassica*

Poppy
Family: Papaveraceae
Genus: *Papaver*

Silver fir
Family: Pinaceae
Genus: *Abies*

Iris
Family: Iridaceae
Genus: *Iris*

Fly agaric (poisonous)
Family: Agaricaceae
Genus: *Amanita*

Water lily
Family: Nymphaeaceae
Genus: *Nymphaea*

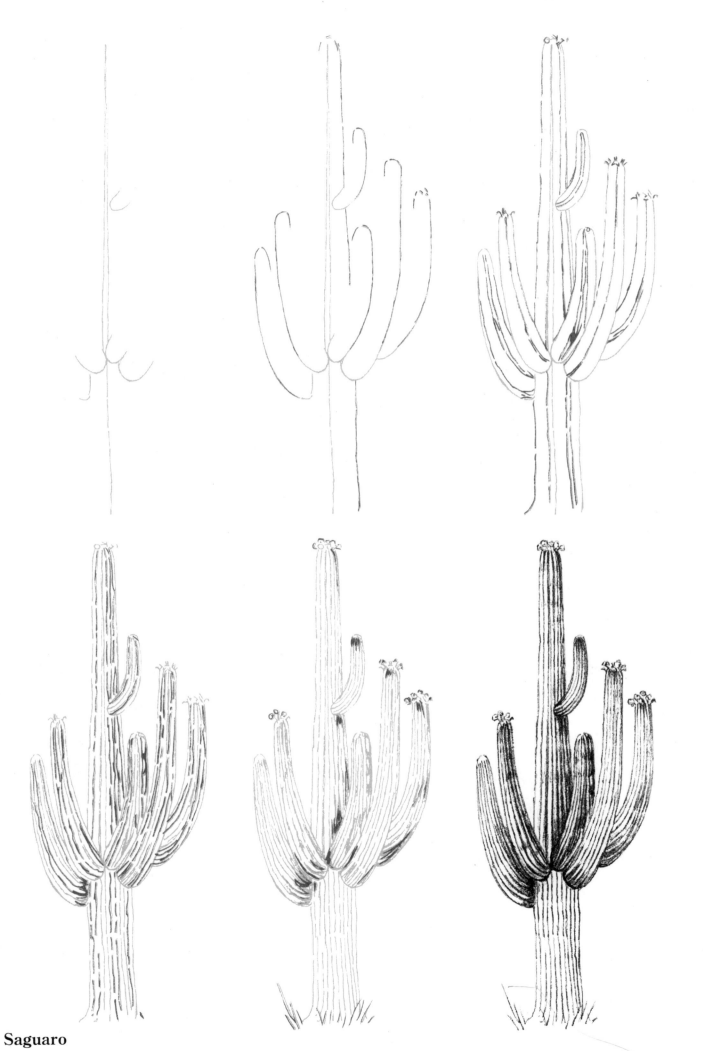

Saguaro
Family: Cactaceae
Genus: *Cereus*

Madonna lily
Family: Liliaceae
Genus: *Lilium*

Skunk cabbage
Family: Araceae
Genus: *Symplocarpus*

Daffodil
Family: Amaryllidaceae
Genus: *Narcissus*

Poinsettia
Family: Euphorbiaceae
Genus: *Euphorbia*

Orange
Family: Rutaceae
Genus: *Citrus*

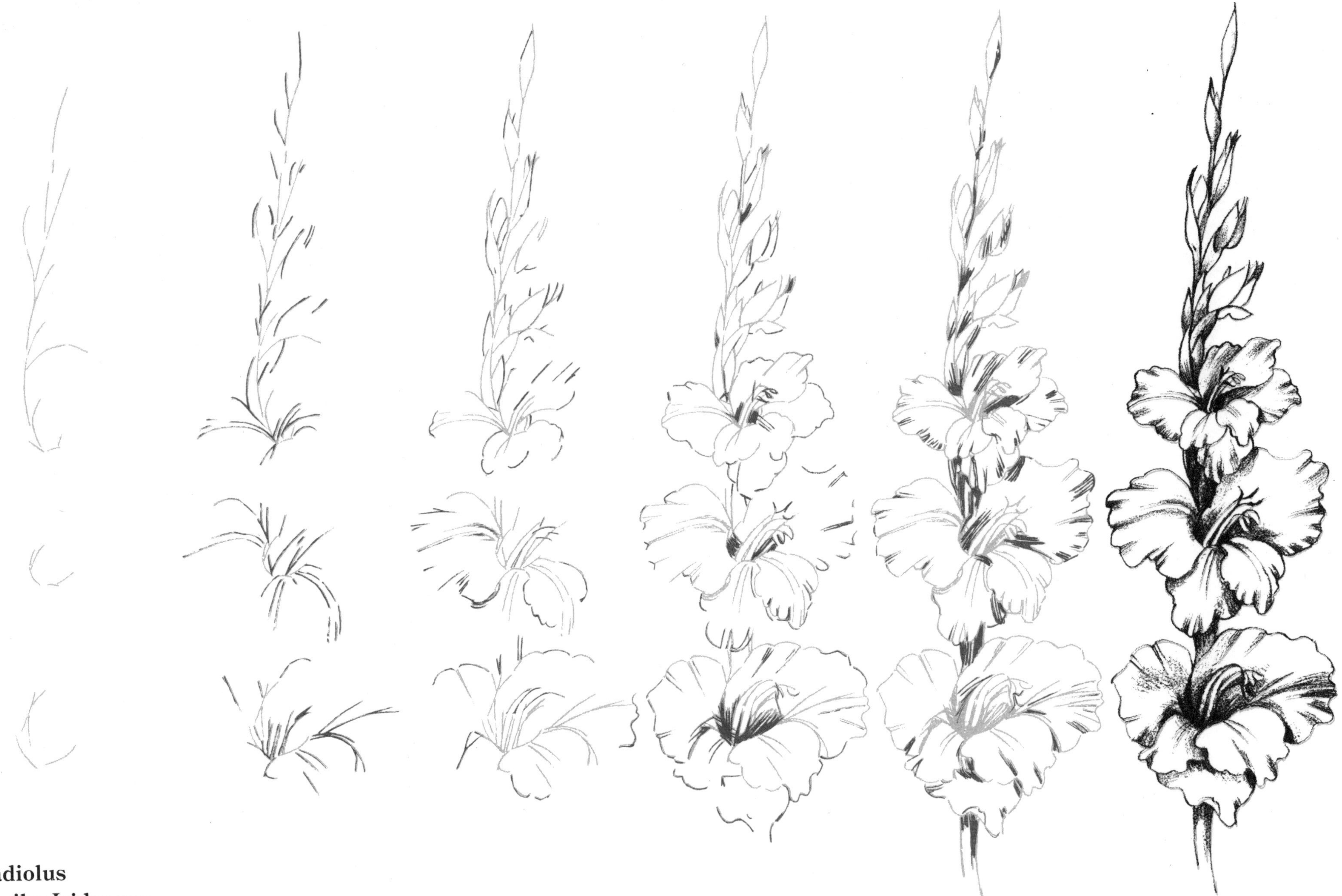

Gladiolus
Family: Iridaceae
Genus: *Gladiolus*

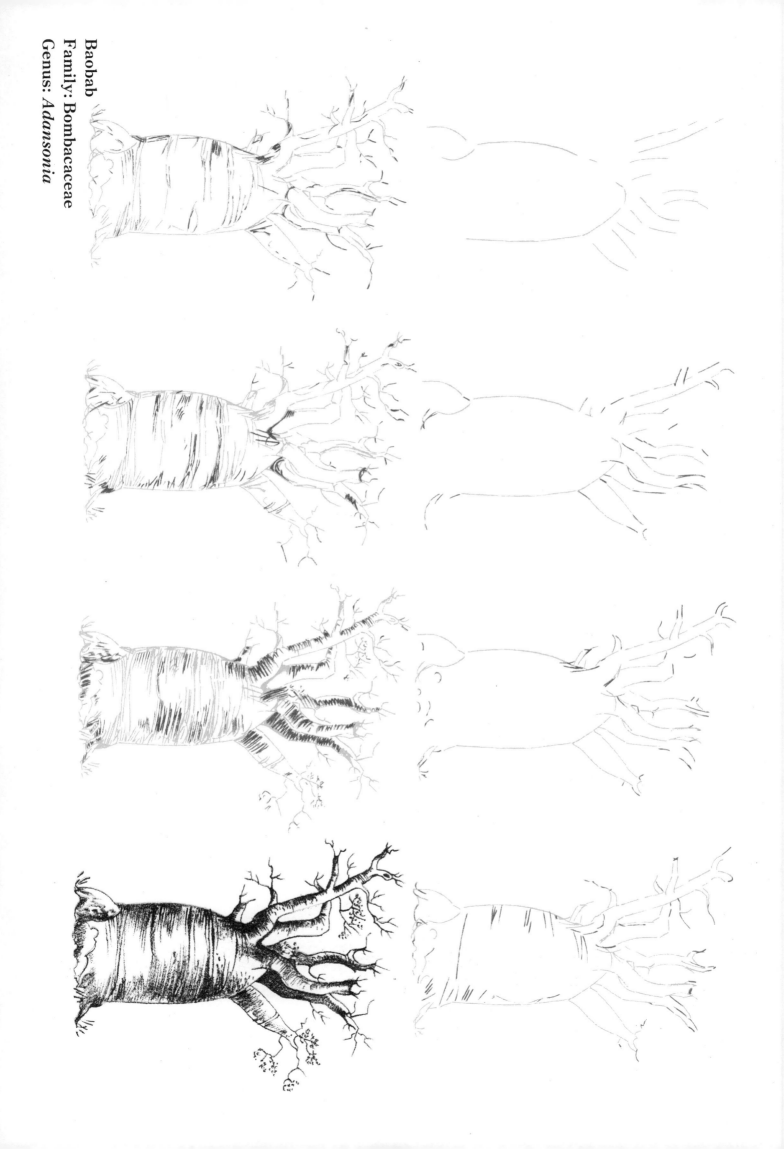

Baobab
Family: Bombacaceae
Genus: *Adansonia*

Narcissus
Family: Amaryllidaceae
Genus: *Narcissus*

Peas
Family: Leguminosae
Genus: *Pisum*

Coconut palm
Family: Palmae
Genus: *Cocos*

Chrysanthemum
Family: Compositae
Genus: *Chrysanthemum*

Grape
Family: Vitaceae
Genus: *Vitis*

Dogwood
Family: Cornaceae
Genus: *Cornus*

Mountain laurel
Family: Ericaceae
Genus: *Kalmia*

Prickly pear
Family: Cactaceae
Genus: *Opuntia*

Giant sequoia
Family: Taxodiaceae
Genus: *Sequoiadendron*

Angel's trumpet
Family: Solanaceae
Genus: *Datura*

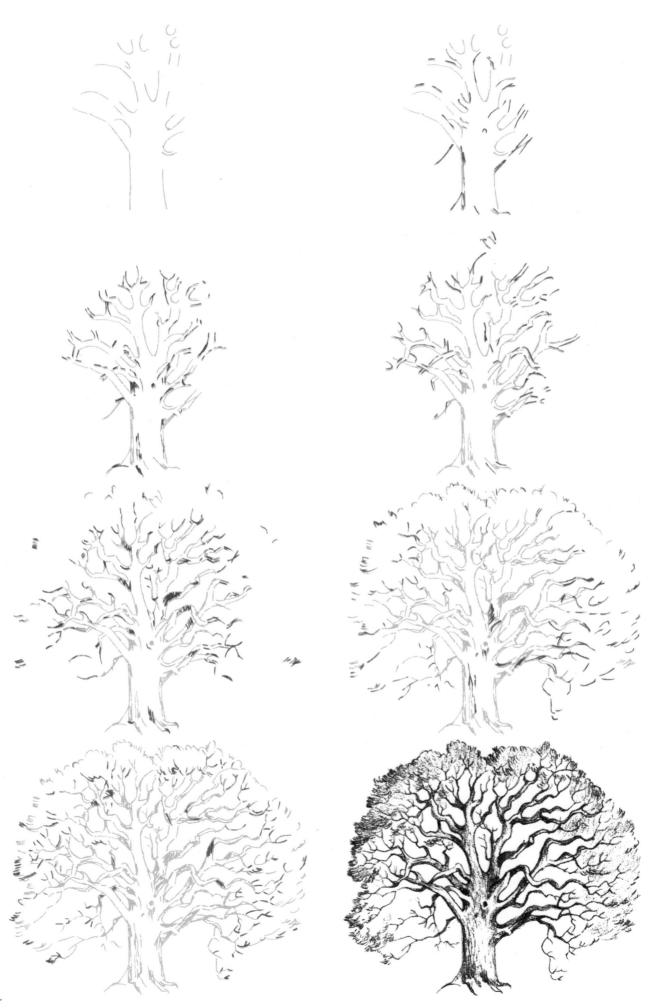

Oak
Family: Fagaceae
Genus: *Quercus*

Orchid
Family: Orchidaceae
Genus: *Cattleya*

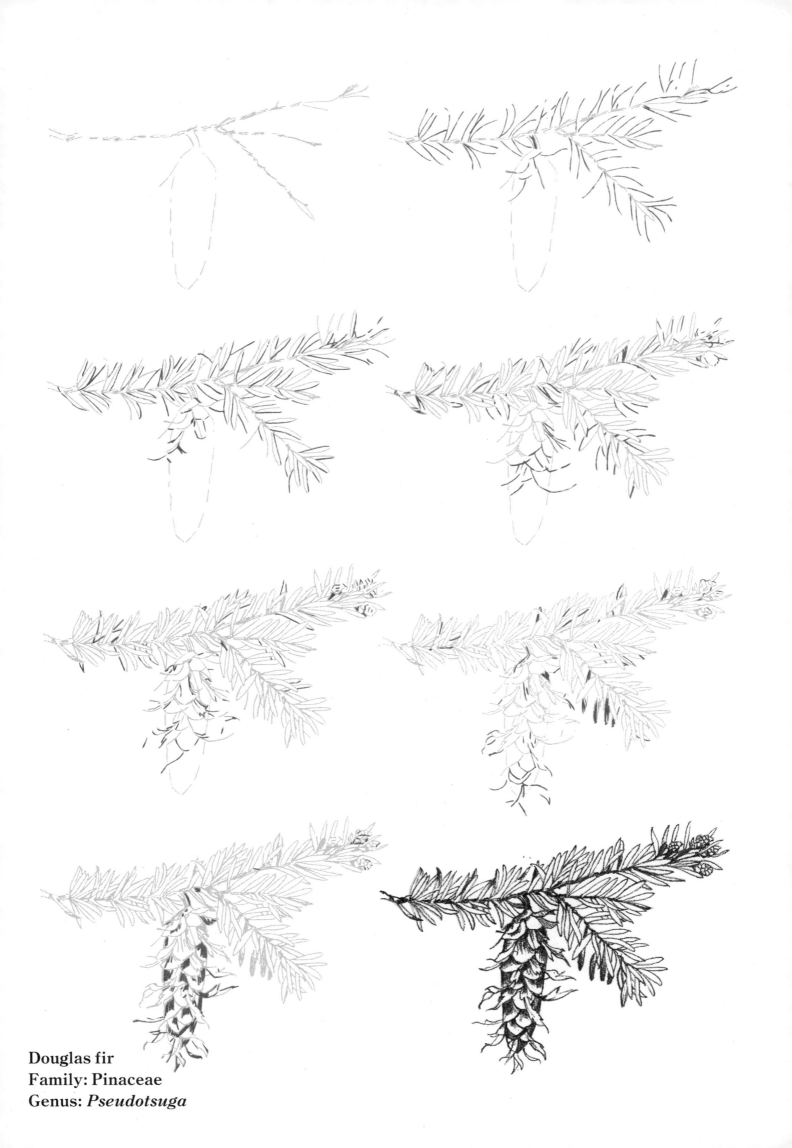

Douglas fir
Family: Pinaceae
Genus: *Pseudotsuga*

Strawberry
Family: Rosaceae
Genus: *Fragaria*

Protea
Family: Proteaceae
Genus: *Protea*

Hollyhock
Family: Malvaceae
Genus: *Althaea*

Chinese lantern
Family: Solanaceae
Genus: *Physalis*

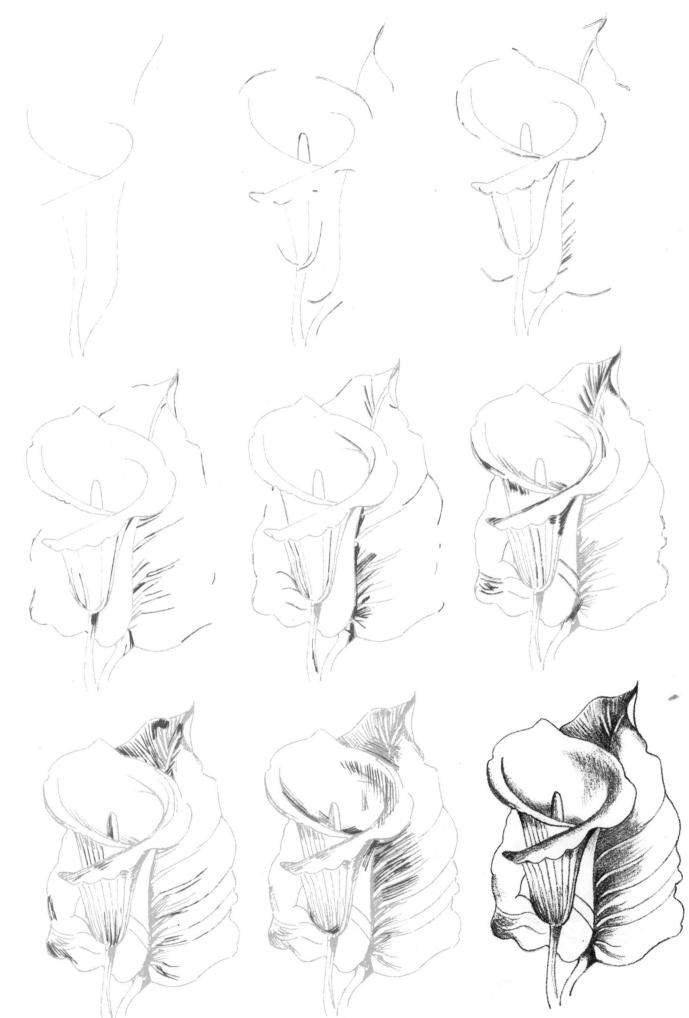

Arum lily
Family: Araceae
Genus: *Zantedeschia*

Holly
Family: Aquifoliaceae
Genus: *Ilex*

Kapok
Family: Bombacaceae
Genus: *Ceiba*

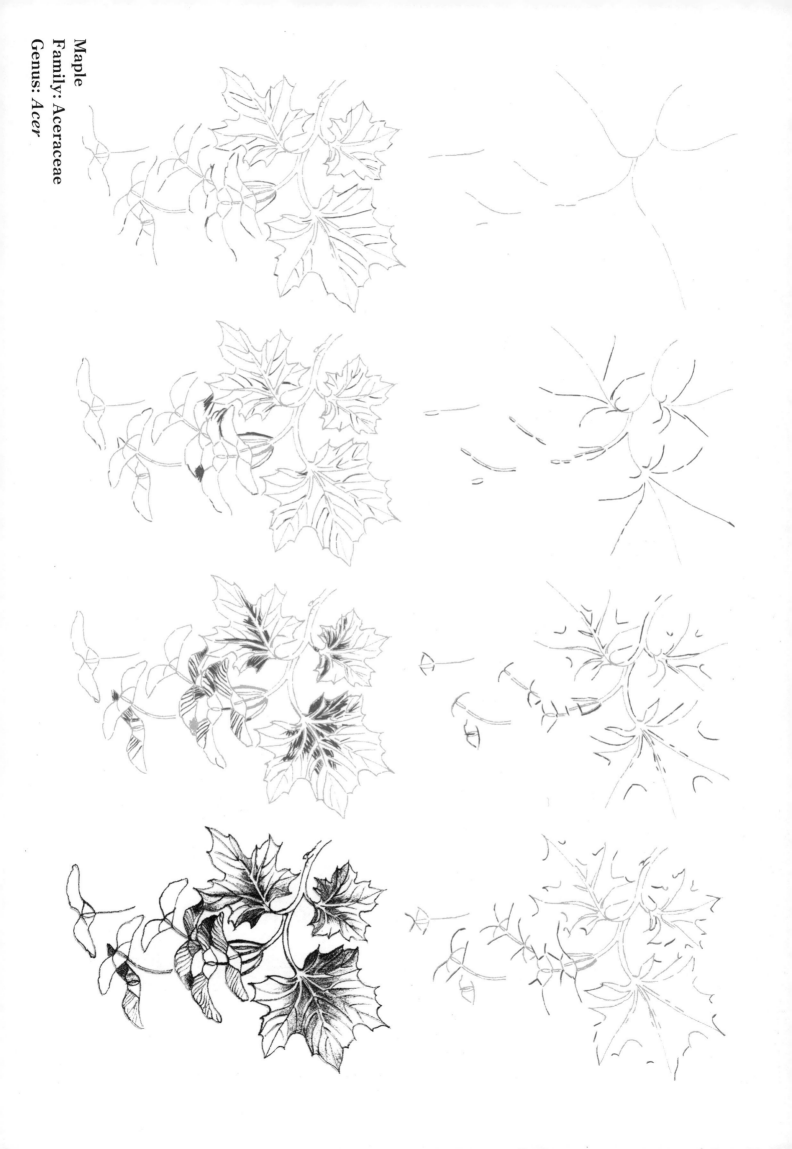

Maple
Family: Aceraceae
Genus: *Acer*

Gloxinia
Family: Gesneriaceae
Genus: *Sinningia*

Lady's slipper
Family: Orchidaceae
Genus: *Cypripedium*

Globe artichoke
Family: Compositae
Genus: *Cynara*

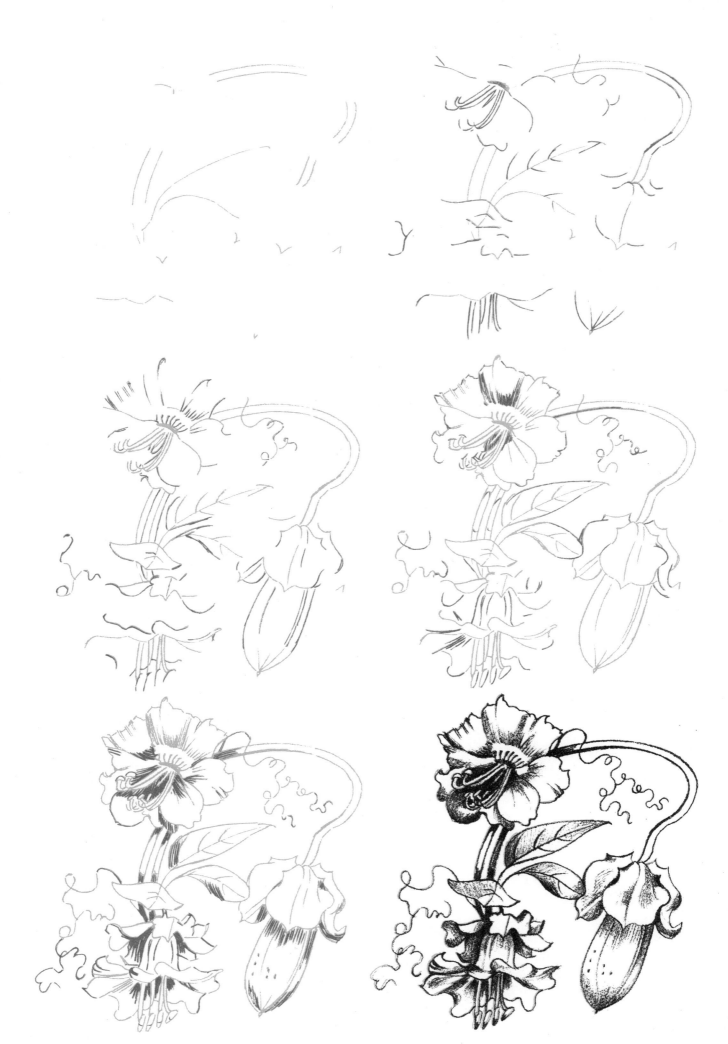

Cup-and-saucer plant
Family: Polemoniaceae
Genus: *Cobaea*

Thistle
Family: Compositae
Genus: *Cirsium*

Pineapple
Family: Bromeliaceae
Genus: *Ananas*

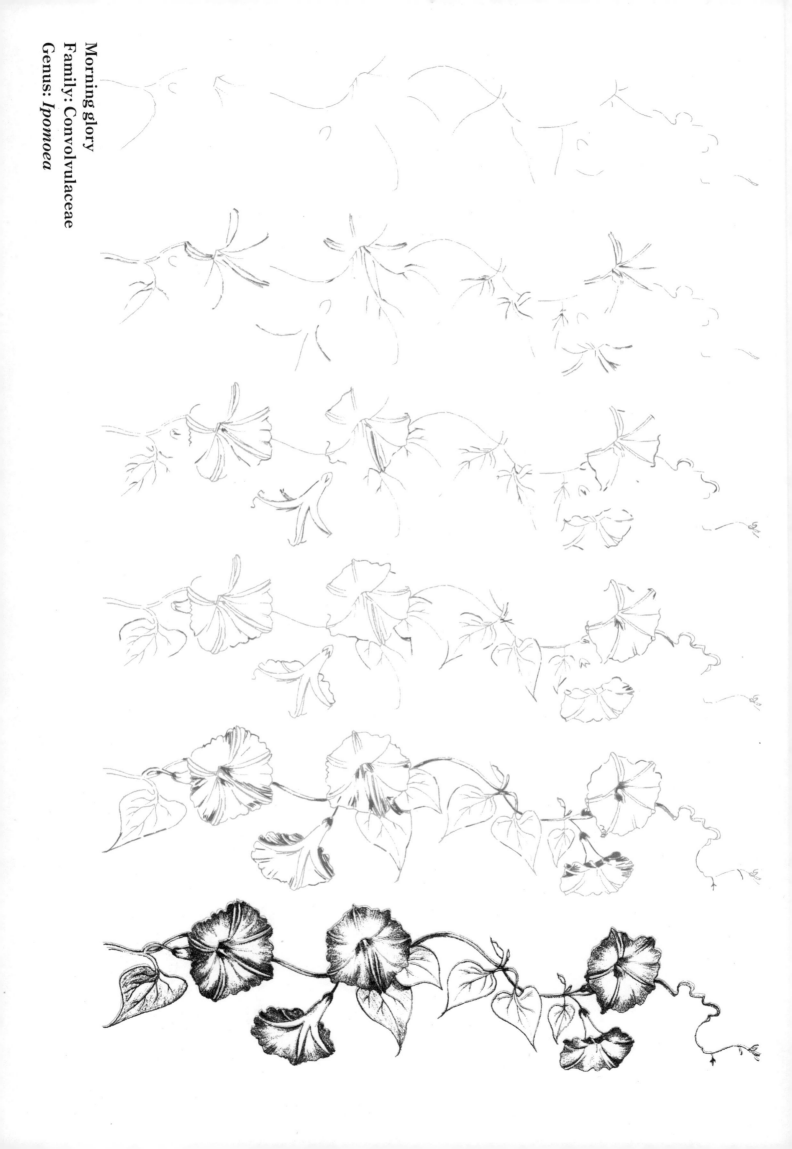

Morning glory
Family: Convolvulaceae
Genus: *Ipomoea*

ABOUT THE AUTHORS

Lee J. Ames has been "drawing 50" since 1974, when the first Draw 50 title – *Draw 50 Animals* – was published. Since that time, Ames has taught millions of people to draw everything from dinosaurs and sharks to boats, buildings and cars.

Peris Lee Ames studied at the Museum of Fine Arts School in Boston and at the Art Students League in New York City. After a professional career in the commercial art field, including advertising, book illustration, jewellery design, and silver and greeting cards for Tiffany & Co., she married and had four children.